MIND DIET ADVANCED

Eat Your Way to Better Brain Health
Recipes and Strategies for the Mind Diet

JOAN JONES

 Copyright © 2024 by Jeffery M. Weaver

ABOUT THE AUTHOR

JOAN JONES Weaver is a dedicated advocate for holistic health and wellness, specializing in the intersection of nutrition and mental health. With a background in mental health counseling and nutrition science, Jeffery brings a unique perspective to his work, emphasizing the powerful connection between diet and emotional well-being.

As a certified nutritionist and licensed mental health counselor, Jeffery has spent years helping individuals improve their mental health through evidence-based nutritional strategies and therapeutic interventions. His integrative approach addresses the complex interplay between diet, brain chemistry, and psychological factors, offering comprehensive support for mental and emotional wellness.

Jones is also a prolific writer and researcher, with a strong commitment to bridging the gap between science and practical application. His articles on nutrition and mental health have been featured in leading publications, providing readers with valuable insights and actionable advice for improving their mental resilience and vitality.

Outside of his professional endeavors, Joan is an enthusiastic advocate for self-care and personal growth. He enjoys sharing his passion for holistic living through workshops, seminars, and community outreach initiatives. Based in Oklahama city, Joan continues to inspire and empower others to cultivate a balanced and fulfilling life rooted in mental well-being and nourishing nutrition and other aspects of human life.

WHAT YOU WILL FIND IN THIS BOOK

INTRODUCTION

1. The Mind-Body Connection and Mental Health.
2. What Is Mind Diet.
3. Potential Benefits Of Mind Diet Mental Wellbeing
4. The Birth of the Mind Diet
5. Structure Of The Book And What To Expect

Chapter 1
Brain Health and Nutrition

1. The Role of Nutrition in Mental Health
2. Specific Impacts on Mental Health
3. Limitation Of Mind Diet

CHAPTER 2
Unveiling The Mind Diet

1. Distinguishing the Mind Diet from the Mediterranean and Dash Diets
2. Scientific Evidence Supporting the MIND Diet and Cognitive Health

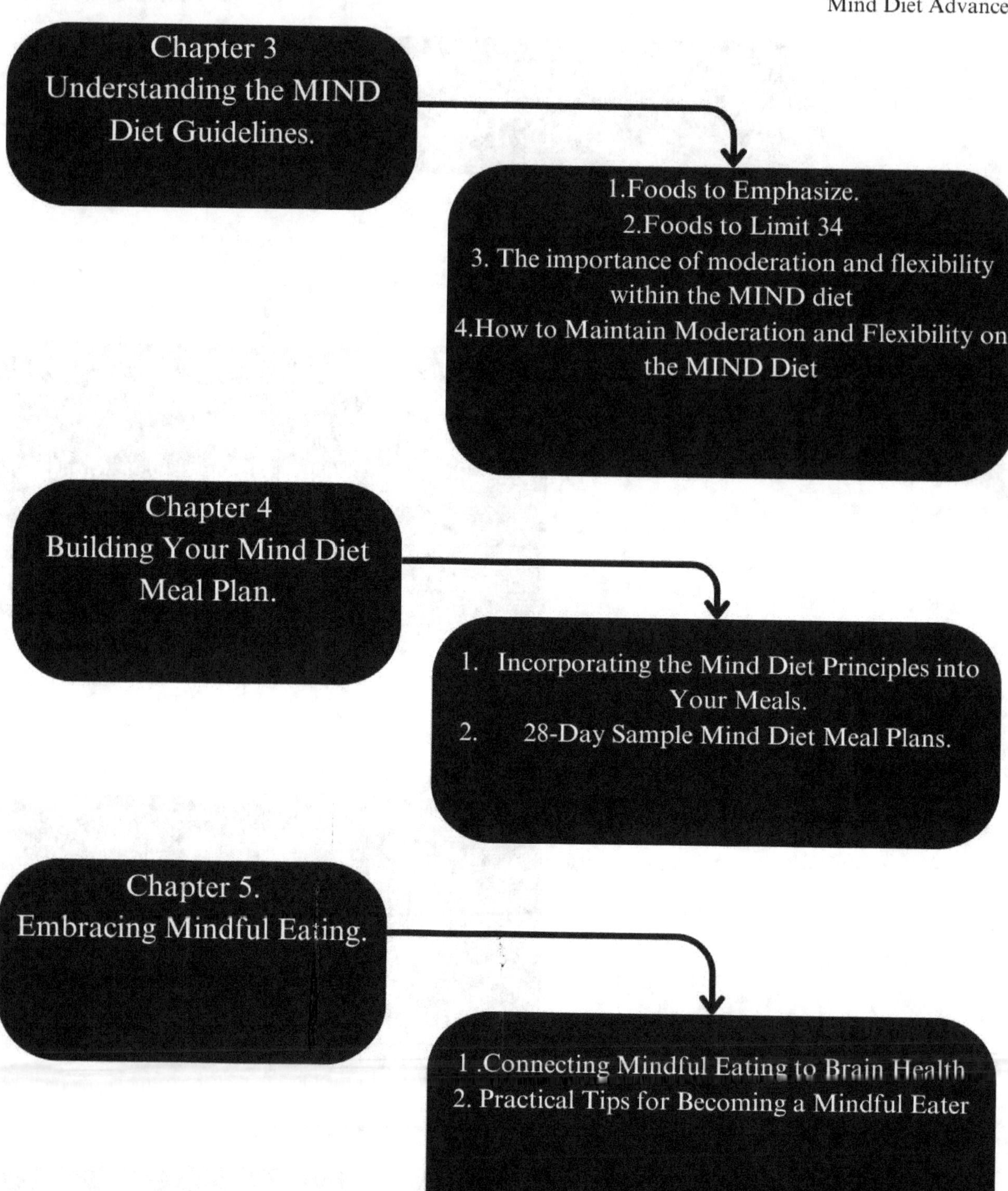

Chapter 3
Understanding the MIND Diet Guidelines.

1.Foods to Emphasize.
2.Foods to Limit 34
3. The importance of moderation and flexibility within the MIND diet
4.How to Maintain Moderation and Flexibility on the MIND Diet

Chapter 4
Building Your Mind Diet Meal Plan.

1. Incorporating the Mind Diet Principles into Your Meals.
2. 28-Day Sample Mind Diet Meal Plans.

Chapter 5.
Embracing Mindful Eating.

1 .Connecting Mindful Eating to Brain Health
2. Practical Tips for Becoming a Mindful Eater

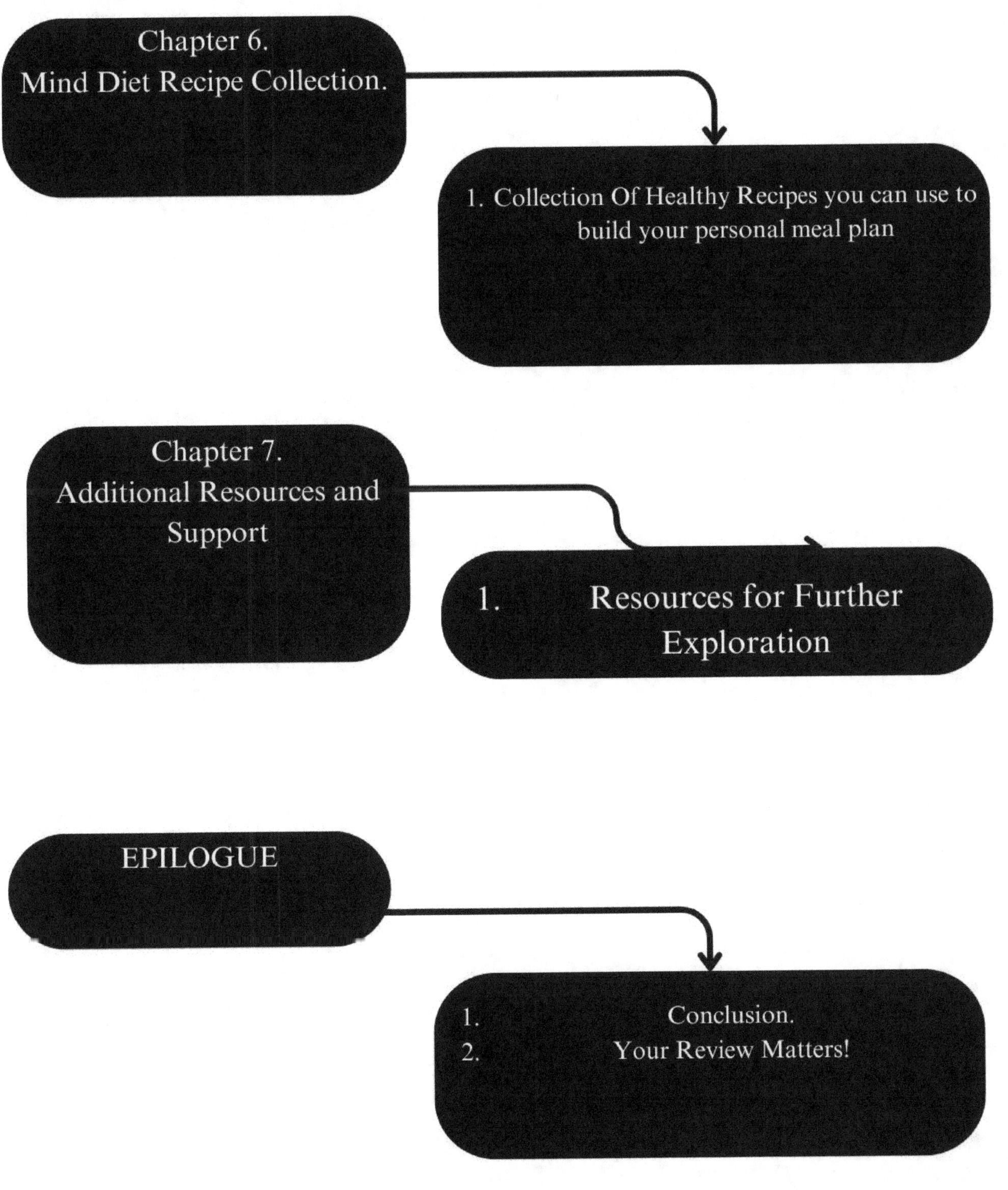
Chapter 6.
Mind Diet Recipe Collection.
1. Collection Of Healthy Recipes you can use to build your personal meal plan
Chapter 7.
Additional Resources and Support
1. Resources for Further Exploration
EPILOGUE
1. Conclusion.
2. Your Review Matters!

❦ Introduction ❧

Have you ever noticed how a bad day can leave you feeling sluggish or how a delicious meal can lift your spirits? This is the power of the mind-body connection, the intricate link between our thoughts, emotions, and physical health. Everything we experience, from our mental state to our diet, impacts our overall well-being.

The Mind-Body Connection and Mental Health
The mind-body connection refers to the intertwined relationship between our thoughts, emotions, and physical health. This means that what happens in our minds can impact our bodies, and vice versa.
Diet plays a significant role in this connection, influencing both our physical and mental well-being. Here's how:

Nutrients: The food we eat provides the building blocks for our brain cells and neurotransmitters, chemicals crucial for mood, memory, and cognitive function. Deficiencies in essential nutrients can contribute to mental health challenges.

Gut health: The gut microbiome, the community of microorganisms in our digestive system, is linked to brain health. Consuming a balanced diet rich in fiber and fermented foods can support a healthy gut microbiome, potentially influencing mood and mental well-being.

Inflammation: Chronic inflammation has been linked to various mental health conditions. Choosing anti-inflammatory foods like fruits, vegetables, and whole grains can help reduce inflammation and potentially benefit mental health.
While diet alone isn't a cure for mental health issues, research suggests that following a healthy eating pattern like the MIND diet, which emphasizes brain-healthy foods, can be a supportive strategy alongside other mental health interventions.

☕ What Is Mind Diet...? ☕

The MIND diet (acronym for Mediterranean-DASH Intervention for Neurodegenerative Delay) is a dietary pattern designed to promote brain health and potentially reduce the risk of dementia and Alzheimer's disease. It was developed by researchers at Rush University Medical Center in Chicago by combining elements from the Mediterranean diet and the DASH diet (Dietary Approaches to Stop Hypertension)

Here's a breakdown of the key points:

Focuses on brain-protective foods: The MIND diet emphasizes foods rich in nutrients believed to benefit brain health,

Limits potentially harmful foods: The diet discourages the consumption of foods associated with an increased risk of cognitive decline

Flexibility: Unlike some diets, the MIND diet doesn't require strict adherence to portion sizes or calorie counting. Instead, it encourages consistent consumption of the recommended foods and limiting the discouraged ones.

While the MIND diet is not a replacement for medical advice or treatment for any mental health condition, research suggests following it closely may be associated with a slower decline in brain function and a lower risk of developing dementia and Alzheimer's disease. This book will provide you with a deeper understanding of the MIND diet and its potential benefits for your brain and overall well-being.

🤲 Benefits Of Mind Diet On Brain Health And Mental 🤲 Wellbeing

1. Enhanced Cognitive Function:

Studies suggest that the Mind diet may be associated with a slower decline in cognitive function and a reduced risk of dementia and Alzheimer's disease.

This link is thought to be due to the presence of specific nutrients found in the diet's recommended foods:

2. Improved Mood:

The Mind diet's emphasis on fruits, vegetables, and whole grains ensures a steady supply of essential nutrients vital for neurotransmitter production.

Neurotransmitters are brain chemicals that regulate mood, and deficiencies can contribute to symptoms of depression and anxiety.

Additionally, the MIND diet's focus on healthy fats and limited processed foods may help regulate blood sugar levels, further contributing to mood stability.

3. Reduced Risk of Depression:

Research suggests a potential link between the MIND diet and a lower risk of depression.

4. Overall Well-being:

By promoting healthy eating habits, the Mind diet indirectly influences mental well-being:

Improved physical health: By promoting overall health and reducing the risk of chronic diseases like diabetes and heart disease, the MIND diet can indirectly contribute to better mental well-being.

Healthy weight management: Maintaining a healthy weight can positively affect mood and self-esteem, impacting overall well-being.

Important Note

While the Mind diet shows promising potential, it's crucial to remember that diet alone isn't a cure for any mental health condition. It's a supportive strategy that should be used in conjunction with other treatment approaches as recommended by healthcare professionals.

⇨ The Birth of the Mind Diet ⇦

In 2015, researchers at Rush University Medical Center in Chicago embarked on a mission to create a dietary plan specifically designed to protect brain health and potentially reduce the risk of dementia and Alzheimer's disease. Led by Dr. Martha Clare Morris, a nutritional epidemiologist, they combined elements from two already established and well-researched dietary patterns:

The Mediterranean diet: Rooted in the traditional eating habits of people living around the Mediterranean Sea, this diet emphasizes fruits, vegetables, whole grains, legumes, fish, and olive oil, with moderate intake of dairy, poultry, and red meat.

The DASH diet (Dietary Approaches to Stop Hypertension): Developed to help lower blood pressure, the DASH diet focuses on fruits, vegetables, whole grains, low-fat dairy products, and limited intake of red meat, added sugars, and saturated fats.

By drawing inspiration from both these diets and incorporating specific recommendations from research on diet and dementia, Dr. Morris and her team created the Mind diet (Mediterranean-DASH Intervention for Neurodegenerative Delay). This unique dietary pattern emphasizes the brain-protective components found in both the Mediterranean and DASH diets, such as:

Leafy green vegetables: Rich in antioxidants and folate, these vegetables may contribute to improved cognitive function.

Berries: Packed with antioxidants, berries may help protect brain cells from damage.

Nuts and seeds: These provide healthy fats, vitamin E, and other nutrients potentially beneficial for brain health.

Whole grains: A source of complex carbohydrates, fiber, and B vitamins, whole grains may support cognitive function and memory.

Get ready to embark on a transformational journey with the MIND diet!

LETS GET STARTED.......!!!

Chapter 1
Brain Health and Nutrition

Our brain, like any other organ in the body, relies heavily on a balanced intake of essential nutrients to function optimally. Deficiencies in these vital components can contribute to various mental health challenges, while a diet rich in the right nutrients can support and promote mental well-being.

Here's a breakdown of some key essential nutrients and their roles in mental health:

1. Omega-3 fatty acids:

Sources: Fatty fish(salmon, tuna, mackerel), nuts(walnuts, flaxseeds), Chia seed

Roles: Play a crucial role in brain cell membrane function, communication, and neurotransmitter production, all of which are essential for mood regulation, learning, and memory. Deficiencies have been linked to depression, anxiety, and cognitive decline.

2. B vitamins:

Sources: Whole grains (brown rice, quinoa), legumes (beans, lentils), leafy green vegetables, eggs, dairy products.

Roles: Crucial for neurotransmitter production, energy metabolism, and cell function within the nervous system. Deficiencies can contribute to symptoms like fatigue, mood swings, difficulty concentrating, and even depression.

3. Choline:

Sources: Eggs, poultry, fish, liver, legumes.

Roles: Essential for building cell membranes and neurotransmitters, particularly acetylcholine, which plays a vital role in memory, learning, and muscle control. Deficiencies have been linked to impaired memory, cognitive decline, and mood problems.

4. Iron:

Sources: Red meat, poultry, beans, lentils, fortified cereals.

Roles: Plays a crucial role in oxygen transport throughout the body, including the brain. Deficiencies can lead to iron deficiency anemia, which can cause fatigue, difficulty concentrating, and low mood.

5. Zinc:

Sources: Oysters, red meat, poultry, nuts, seeds, whole grains.

Roles: Involved in neurotransmitter production, brain development, and immune function. Deficiencies have been linked to depression, anxiety, and impaired cognitive function.

6. Magnesium:

Sources: Leafy green vegetables, nuts, seeds, whole grains, legumes.

Roles: Involved in over 300 biochemical reactions in the body, including those related to neurotransmission, muscle function, and energy production. Deficiencies can contribute to anxiety, insomnia, and difficulty concentrating.

7. Vitamin D:

Sources: Fatty fish, egg yolks, fortified foods (milk, cereal), sunlight exposure.

Roles: Acts as a hormone and plays a role in brain development, neurotransmitter function, and immune regulation. Deficiencies have been linked to depression, anxiety, and seasonal affective disorder (SAD).

8. Folate:

Sources: Leafy green vegetables, legumes, fruits, fortified foods (bread, cereal).
Roles: Crucial for DNA synthesis, cell division, and neurotransmitter production. Deficiencies have been linked to depression, anxiety, and cognitive decline.

9. Antioxidant

Sources: in fruits, vegetables, and whole grains)
Role : Help protect brain cells from damage caused by free radicals, which are unstable molecules linked to aging and neurodegenerative diseases.
This list is not exhaustive, and other nutrients also play important roles in mental health. Consulting a healthcare professional or registered dietitian is crucial for personalized dietary guidance tailored to your specific needs and health conditions.

The Role of Nutrition in Supporting Brain Function and Mental Health

1. Building Blocks for Brain Structure:

Omega-3 fatty acids: These essential fats, particularly DHA and EPA, are crucial for building and maintaining healthy neuron membranes. These membranes act as the "gatekeepers" of neurons, controlling the flow of information and influencing communication between brain cells. Deficiencies in omega-3s have been linked to impaired cognitive function, memory problems, and an increased risk of neurodegenerative diseases like Alzheimer's.

Myelin formation: Myelin acts like a protective and insulating sheath around nerve fibers, allowing for faster and more efficient signal transmission between neurons. Healthy fats, along with B vitamins and choline, play a vital role in the production and maintenance of myelin. Myelin damage can cause various neurological problems, including numbness, weakness, and difficulty with coordination.

2. Energy Supply for Optimal Function:

Complex carbohydrates: Unlike simple sugars found in processed foods and sugary drinks, complex carbohydrates from whole grains, fruits, and legumes provide a sustained release of glucose into the bloodstream. This ensures a steady supply of energy for the brain to function optimally, promoting alertness, focus, and cognitive performance. Conversely, fluctuations in blood sugar caused by simple sugars can lead to fatigue, difficulty concentrating, and mood swings.

Essential amino acids: Protein is broken down into amino acids, which are the building blocks of protein and serve various functions within the brain. Some specific amino acids like tryptophan are precursors to neurotransmitters such as serotonin, which plays a role in mood regulation and sleep. Adequate protein intake is crucial for supporting various brain functions.

3. Neurotransmitter Production:

B vitamins: These vitamins are essential for synthesizing various neurotransmitters, including acetylcholine (involved in memory and learning), serotonin (regulates mood and sleep), and dopamine (associated with reward and motivation). Deficiencies in B vitamins can lead to imbalances in these neurotransmitters, contributing to symptoms of depression, anxiety, and cognitive decline.

Choline: This crucial nutrient is involved in the production of acetylcholine, a neurotransmitter essential for memory, learning, and muscle control. Deficiencies in choline have been linked to impaired memory, cognitive decline, and an increased risk of Alzheimer's disease.

Iron and zinc: These minerals play a vital role in various biochemical reactions within the brain, including neurotransmitter production. Deficiencies in iron and zinc have been associated with impaired cognitive function, mood problems, and an increased risk of depression.

4. Protection Against Damage:

Antioxidants: These compounds found in fruits, vegetables, and whole grains help combat oxidative stress caused by free radicals, which can damage brain cells and contribute to cognitive decline and neurodegenerative diseases. Vitamin C, vitamin E, and beta-carotene are some essential antioxidant nutrients.

Inflammation: Chronic inflammation has been linked to various brain disorders, including depression, anxiety, and Alzheimer's disease. Diets rich in anti-inflammatory foods like fruits, vegetables, and whole grains can help reduce inflammation and potentially benefit brain health.

Specific Impacts on Mental Health

Cognitive Function and Decline: Studies suggest that a Mediterranean diet, rich in fruits, vegetables, whole grains, olive oil, and fish, may be associated with a slower decline in cognitive function and a reduced risk of dementia and Alzheimer's disease. Additionally, specific nutrients like vitamin E have been shown to potentially benefit memory and cognitive function in older adults.

Mood Regulation: Research indicates that deficiencies in vitamin D may be linked to an increased risk of depression. Conversely, studies suggest that consuming foods rich in omega-3 fatty acids may have mood-boosting effects and potentially help manage symptoms of depression.

Neurodevelopment: Maternal nutrition during pregnancy plays a crucial role in fetal brain development. Deficiencies in essential nutrients like iron can have long-lasting consequences, impacting cognitive function and increasing the risk of mental health challenges later in life.

Gut-Brain Connection: The gut microbiome, the community of bacteria residing in the gut, impacts various aspects of our health, including mental well-being. A diverse and balanced gut microbiome has been linked to improved mood and reduced risk of depression and anxiety. Consuming probiotics (found in fermented foods like yogurt and kefir) and prebiotics (found in dietary fiber) can promote a healthy gut microbiome.

Remember

While specific nutrients play important roles, it's the overall dietary pattern that matters most. A balanced and varied diet rich in whole foods is crucial for optimal brain health and mental well-being.

Individual needs can vary, and consulting with a healthcare professional or registered dietitian

Limitation Of Mind Diet

It's crucial to acknowledge the limitations of relying solely on diet for improved mental health. While the MIND diet and other dietary approaches show promising potential in supporting brain health, several other factors play significant roles: Genetics: Certain genetic predispositions can influence risk for mental health conditions.

Underlying medical conditions: In some cases, mental health challenges can be linked to underlying medical conditions that require medical intervention.

Therefore, it's essential to adopt a holistic approach to mental well-being, addressing various aspects of your life alongside exploring dietary strategies like the Mind diet. Consulting a healthcare professional for personalized guidance and addressing potential underlying causes remains crucial.

In addition to nutrition, other lifestyle factors such as sleep, exercise, stress management, and genetics also exert profound influences on our mental health and cognitive function. Neglecting these factors can undermine even the most well-crafted dietary regimen.

Quality sleep is essential for brain health, as it allows for restorative processes such as memory consolidation and neural repair. Regular physical activity not only improves blood flow to the brain but also promotes the release of neurotransmitters and growth factors that support mood regulation and cognitive function.

Effective stress management techniques, such as mindfulness meditation or deep breathing exercises, can help mitigate the harmful effects of chronic stress on the brain and mental well-being. Additionally, acknowledging the role of genetics in predisposing individuals to certain mental health conditions underscores the importance of personalized approaches to mental wellness.

CHAPTER 2
Unveiling The Mind Diet

Research Focus: The Mind diet was developed by researchers at Rush University Medical Center in Chicago, specifically Dr. Martha Clare Morris and her team. Their primary goal was to investigate the relationship between diet and cognitive decline in the aging population.

Rationale: Researchers recognized a significant link between nutritional deficiencies and cognitive decline. However, existing dietary patterns like the Mediterranean and Dash diets, while beneficial, didn't specifically target nutrients and food groups most closely associated with brain health and protection against neurodegenerative diseases.

The Birth of Mind: The Mind diet was the result of meticulous research into identifying specific foods and dietary patterns linked to
·**Reduced risk of cognitive decline**
·**Decreased risk of Alzheimer's disease**
·**Improved cognitive function and mental well-being**

Purpose of the Mind Diet

The primary purpose of the Mind diet is to promote brain health and potentially reduce the risk of cognitive decline and neurodegenerative diseases like Alzheimer's. It accomplishes this by focusing on incorporating foods and dietary patterns that have been scientifically linked to neuro-protective benefits.

Elaborating on the MIND Diet

Hybrid Approach: The MIND diet merges two well-established dietary patterns which includes

1. Mediterranean diet: Known for its emphasis on fruits, vegetables, whole grains, fish, olive oil, and moderate intake of wine.
2. DASH diet: Developed for reducing hypertension (high blood pressure) by focusing on fruits, vegetables, whole grains, low-fat dairy, and limited salt intake.

Distinguishing the Mind Diet from the Mediterranean and Dash Diets

While the Mind diet shares some similarities with its parent diets, the Mediterranean and DASH, it possesses unique features designed specifically to target brain health and potentially reduce the risk of cognitive decline. Here's a detailed comparison

Origins

MIND: Developed by Dr. Martha Clare Morris et al. at Rush University Medical Center based on research linking specific foods to brain health.

Mediterranean: Traditional dietary pattern observed in countries bordering the Mediterranean Sea, known for its heart-healthy characteristics.

DASH: Developed by the National Institutes of Health to lower blood pressure.

Focus:

MIND: Primarily focuses on brain health and cognitive function, promoting foods with neuro-protective properties while limiting those potentially harmful.

Mediterranean: Emphasizes overall health and longevity, promoting a heart-healthy pattern rich in fruits, vegetables, whole grains, olive oil, and moderate wine intake.

DASH: Primarily focuses on lowering blood pressure, emphasizing fruits, vegetables, whole grains, low-fat dairy, and limited sodium intake.

Food Groups

MIND:

Emphasis: Leafy green vegetables, berries, nuts, whole grains, fish, poultry, olive oil.

Limitation: Red meat, butter/cheese, fried foods, sweets, pastries.

Mediterranean:

Key elements: Fruits, vegetables, whole grains, legumes, olive oil, fish, moderate intake of wine, poultry, and dairy (including cheese).

Red meat: Limited consumption compared to MIND.

DASH:

Similar to Mediterranean in fruits, vegetables, whole grains, and legumes.

Focuses on low-fat and fat-free dairy products.

Stricter limitations on sodium intake compared to both MIND and Mediterranean.

Unique Features of the Mind Diet

Strong emphasis on specific brain-healthy foods: Berries, leafy green vegetables, nuts. Stricter limitations on specific foods linked to poorer cognitive outcomes: Red meat, saturated and trans fats from fried foods and pastries, sweets.

Flexibility: Encourages incorporating recommended foods as frequently as possible while allowing individual customization.

Focuses on dietary patterns over strict rules: Encourages overall healthy eating habits with an emphasis on specific brain-supportive foods.

Similarities between the three diets

All emphasize fruits, vegetables, and whole grains.
All encourage limiting processed foods, sugary drinks, and unhealthy fats.
All promote moderate alcohol consumption (except for DASH, which recommends limited intake).

Scientific Evidence Supporting the MIND Diet and Cognitive Health

The Mind diet has gained significant attention for its potential to promote brain health and potentially reduce the risk of cognitive decline and neurodegenerative diseases like Alzheimer's and dementia. While the research is ongoing, several studies provide compelling evidence suggesting a link between adherence to the MIND diet and improved cognitive outcomes.

Key Observational Studies

1. Rush University Medical Center Study (2006): This pioneering study, conducted by Dr. Martha Clare Morris et al., followed over 1,200 elderly individuals for four years. They found that higher adherence to the MIND diet was associated with a slower decline in cognitive function, suggesting a potential protective effect against cognitive decline.

2. French Study (2017): This study, involving over 700 adults, observed that closer adherence to the MIND diet was associated with better cognitive performance, particularly in memory and executive function.

3. Australian Study (2019): This study, which included over 1,500 participants, found that individuals with higher MIND diet scores had improved cognitive function, particularly in verbal memory and processing speed.

Potential Mechanisms of Action

These studies suggest a potential association between the MIND diet and cognitive health. However, researchers are still unraveling the precise mechanisms behind this connection. Some potential mechanisms include:

Increased intake of brain-healthy nutrients: The MIND diet emphasizes foods rich in essential vitamins and minerals like folate, vitamin E, and B vitamins, crucial for neurotransmitter production, brain cell function, and protection from oxidative damage.

Reduced intake of potentially harmful foods: The MIND diet limits saturated and trans fats, processed foods, and sugary drinks, all of which have been linked to inflammation and impaired cognitive function.

Promoting gut health: The Mind diet may support a healthy gut microbiome, which has been increasingly recognized as playing a role in brain health and cognitive function.

Limitations and Future Directions

It's important to acknowledge the limitations of the current evidence:

Observational studies: These studies cannot definitively establish cause-and-effect relationships between the MIND diet and cognitive health. Other factors might influence observed associations.

Need for larger and longer-term studies: More research with larger participant pools and longer follow-up periods is needed to confirm and fully understand the long-term impact of the MIND diet on cognitive function.

Despite these limitations, the existing research suggests a promising link between the MIND diet and cognitive health. As research progresses, we can expect a deeper understanding of the mechanisms involved and the potential long-term benefits of this dietary approach for promoting brain health and potentially reducing the risk of cognitive decline.

Chapter 3
Understanding the MIND Diet Guidelines

Foods to Emphasize

Leafy Green Vegetables (1 serving daily): Packed with vital nutrients like folate, vitamins E and K, and carotenoids, these vegetables play a potential role in protecting brain cells from age-related damage and neurodegeneration. Examples include kale, spinach, collard greens, and Swiss chard.

Berries (2-3 servings weekly): Rich in anthocyanins (powerful antioxidants), berries may have anti-inflammatory and neuroprotective effects, potentially reducing the risk of cognitive decline. Blueberries, strawberries, and raspberries are excellent choices.

Nuts (5 servings weekly): A good source of healthy fats, vitamin E, and omega-3 fatty acids, nuts may contribute to improved cognitive function mind memory. Almonds, walnuts, cashews, and pistachios are good options.

Whole Grains (3 servings daily): Whole grains provide sustained energy and are rich in fiber and B vitamins, crucial for neurotransmitter production and brain function. Opt for brown rice, quinoa, whole-wheat bread, and oats.

Fish (once weekly): Rich in omega-3 fatty acids, particularly DHA, fish consumption has been linked to improved cognitive function and reduced risk of dementia. Fatty fish like salmon, mackerel, herring, and sardines are preferred.

Poultry (2 servings weekly): Poultry is a lean protein source that provides essential amino acids needed for neurotransmitter production and brain cell function. Chicken and turkey are good choices.

Olive Oil (primary source of added fat): Olive oil is rich in monounsaturated fats, which may have neuroprotective properties and contribute to healthy blood flow to the brain. Use it for cooking, salad dressings, and marinades.

Foods to Limit

Red Meat (less than once weekly): Excessive red meat consumption has been linked to increased inflammation and potentially higher risks of cognitive decline and dementia. It's recommended to choose lean cuts and moderate your intake.

Butter and Cheese (less than 5 servings weekly): While dairy products provide essential nutrients like calcium, saturated fat intake from excessive butter and cheese consumption may be detrimental to brain health. Opt for low-fat dairy options and prioritize other sources of healthy fats like olive oil and nuts.

Fried Foods and Pastries (less than once weekly): These foods are typically high in saturated and trans fats, which may contribute to inflammation and potentially increase the risk of cognitive decline. Limit French fries, fried chicken, pastries, and donuts.

Sweets and Sugary Drinks (rarely or not at all): Sugary drinks and processed sweets can lead to spikes in blood sugar levels, impacting brain function and potentially contributing to cognitive decline. Limit sugary sodas, juices, candy, and commercially baked goods.

The importance of moderation and flexibility within the MIND diet

1. Moderation Promotes Sustainability:

Avoiding Extremes: The MIND diet differentiates itself from rigid diets by encouraging moderation. This approach prevents feelings of deprivation and potential burnout, promoting long-term adherence.

Occasional Indulgences: Allowing for flexibility accommodates occasional treats or indulgences within an overall healthy eating pattern. This eliminates the guilt or "all-or-nothing" mindset that can derail healthy eating efforts.

Balance: Emphasizing moderation creates a sense of balance. It prioritizes maximizing brain-healthy foods while allowing for realistic adaptations and mindful choices.

2. Flexibility Ensures Personalization and Enjoyment:

Adaptations for Preferences: Flexibility allows for individual preferences and dislikes, making the diet more enjoyable and adaptable to personal needs.

Cultural Differences: Dietary patterns can vary widely across cultures. The MIND diet's flexibility allows for incorporating culturally relevant healthy foods.

Lifestyle Considerations: Whether it's a busy schedule or food allergies, flexibility allows for adjustments that fit into your unique lifestyle and circumstances. This makes the diet more sustainable in the long run.

How to Maintain Moderation and Flexibility on the MIND Diet

Focus on Progress, Not Perfection: Aim for gradual changes and celebrate your progress rather than striving for unrealistic perfection.

Plan Ahead: Plan your meals and snacks to ensure you have healthy options available that align with the MIND diet's principles.

Mindful Eating: Practice mindful eating and pay attention to your body's hunger and fullness cues. Enjoy your food without judgment.

Seek Support: Connect with a registered dietitian or healthcare professional for personalized guidance and support in creating a flexible approach while adhering to the core principles of the diet.

Chapter 4
Building Your Mind Diet Meal Plan

Here's a guide on creating personalized meal plans based on preferences and dietary restrictions while maintaining the principles of the MIND diet:

Step 1: Assess Your Needs and Preferences

Dietary Requirements: Start by listing your dietary restrictions (allergies, intolerances, medical conditions) for non-negotiable exclusions.

Taste Preferences: List foods you love and ones you dislike within the MIND-recommended categories. Include preferred cuisines or cooking styles.

Lifestyle Factors: Consider your cooking skills, schedule (how much time you have for preparation), and budget.

Step 2: Find Substitutions (If Needed)

Allergies/Intolerances: Identify suitable replacements within allowed MIND food categories. For example, if you have lactose intolerance, choose plant-based milk and yogurt or low-lactose options.

Dislikes: Explore alternatives within the same food group. For example, if you dislike kale, try spinach, collard greens, or Swiss chard.

Step 3: Focus on MIND-Friendly Foods

Build Your Menu: Create a list of preferred foods from each emphasized MIND category

Step 4: Meal Planning

Build a Meal Template: Design a rough structure for your days (e.g., breakfast, lunch, dinner, snacks) to simplify planning.

Seek Inspiration: Explore MIND-friendly recipes online or in cookbooks. Find sources with adaptations or substitution tips for dietary restrictions.

Variety: Incorporate diverse meals throughout the week to keep it interesting and ensure good nutrient intake.

Start Simple: Initially, focus on incorporating more MIND-friendly foods into your usual meals before creating complex new recipes.

Step 5: Be Flexible and Adjust

Monitor and Tweak: Track how you feel after meals and adjust your choices.

Don't Give Up: It takes time to adapt to new eating habits. Celebrate small wins and don't focus on perfection.

Seek Support: Consider working with a registered dietitian to personalize the plan and troubleshoot challenges.

Helpful Tips

Grocery Lists: Plan your shopping according to your meal plan, and keep MIND-friendly staples on hand.

Portion Control: Be mindful of portion sizes, even with healthy choices.

Cook in Batches: Prepare components in advance for easy meals throughout the week.

Explore New Flavors: Challenge yourself to try different recipes and ingredients within the MIND framework.

Remember: Creating a personalized meal plan on the MIND diet is an ongoing process. Incorporate your individuality, experiment, and stay consistent with the core principles. Be patient, seek support when needed, and enjoy the journey to better health!

Incorporating the Mind Diet Principles into Your Meals

The MIND diet emphasizes specific foods that can contribute to brain health. Here's how to incorporate these principles into your daily meals and snacks.

BREAKFAST OPTIONS

Go whole-grain:

Choose whole-wheat toast, oatmeal, or brown rice porridge.

Add berries:

Top your cereal with berries like strawberries or blueberries, or add them to a smoothie.

Include nuts:

Add almonds, walnuts, or chia seeds to your oatmeal or yogurt for a protein and healthy fat boost.

Opt for brain-healthy fats:

Drizzle olive oil on your toast or enjoy avocado toast with a sprinkle of berries.

Limit sugary cereals and pastries:

Choose healthier alternatives like whole-wheat pancakes with berries or a protein smoothie.

LUNCH OPTIONS

Build a salad:

Start with a base of leafy greens and add protein options like grilled chicken or fish, lentils, or beans. Include vegetables like tomatoes, cucumber, and carrots. Top with a vinaigrette dressing made with olive oil.

Leftovers become lunch:

Opt for leftover salmon from dinner with a side of brown rice or whole-wheat pasta.

Soup and whole-grain bread:

Enjoy lentil soup or vegetable minestrone with whole-wheat bread for a satisfying and fiber-rich lunch.

Wrap it up!:

Make a whole-wheat wrap with grilled chicken, hummus, and vegetables like spinach and bell peppers.

Avoid processed lunches: Limit pre-packaged sandwiches, fried foods, and sugary drinks.

DINNER OPTIONS

Baked or grilled fish:

Opt for salmon, tuna, or mackerel baked with herbs and lemon, or grilled with vegetables like broccoli or asparagus.

Roasted chicken:

Roast chicken with vegetables like sweet potatoes, carrots, and onions for a complete and healthy meal.

Vegetarian options:

Enjoy lentil or bean-based dishes like lentil soup, chili, or vegetarian burgers with whole-wheat buns.

Whole-grain side dishes:

Include brown rice, quinoa, or whole-wheat pasta alongside your main course.

Limit red meat:

Reduce your red meat intake to a serving or less per week. Opt for lean cuts and healthy cooking methods like grilling or baking.

Minimize fried foods:

Enjoy fried foods sparingly and focus on healthier cooking methods like roasting, baking, or grilling.

SNACKS OPTIONS

Fruits and nuts:

Snack on berries, apples, oranges, or other fruits combined with a handful of almonds, walnuts, or cashews.

Veggies and hummus:

Enjoy carrot sticks, cucumber slices, or bell pepper slices with hummus for a filling and nutritious snack.

Yogurt with nuts and berries:

Choose plain yogurt and top it with berries and a sprinkle of nuts for a satisfying snack.

Hard-boiled egg:

Enjoy a hard-boiled egg for a protein-packed snack.

Trail mix:

Make your own trail mix using nuts, seeds, and dried fruits (choose unsweetened varieties).

Avoid sugary snacks:

Limit sugary treats like cookies, cakes, and candy. Opt for healthier alternatives like fruits or yogurt.

Remember:

These are just suggestions, feel free to experiment and find what works best for your preferences and lifestyle.

Be mindful of portion sizes, even with healthy foods.

Cooking at home allows you to control the ingredients and ensure a balanced and healthy meal.

28-Day Sample Mind Diet Meal Plans

WEEK 1

DAY 1

Breakfast: Oatmeal with berries and chia seeds

Lunch: Salad with grilled chicken, quinoa, and a vinaigrette dressing

Dinner: Baked salmon with roasted vegetables (asparagus, Brussels sprouts) and brown rice

Snacks: Apple slices with almond butter, carrot sticks with hummus

DAY 2

Breakfast: Smoothie with almond milk, banana, spinach, and protein powder

Lunch: Lentil soup with whole-wheat bread

Dinner: Veggie stir-fry with tofu and brown rice noodles

Snacks: Berries with a handful of almonds, hard-boiled egg with cucumber slices

DAY 3

Breakfast: Whole-wheat pancakes with blueberries and walnuts

Lunch: Chickpea salad sandwich on whole-wheat bread with avocado and lettuce

Dinner: Baked chicken with roasted vegetables (sweet potatoes, carrots, broccoli) and quinoa

Snacks: Trail mix with nuts, seeds, and dried fruits, Greek yogurt with berries and chia seeds

DAY 4

Breakfast: Scrambled eggs with spinach and salsa

Lunch: Leftover salmon from dinner with a side of brown rice

Dinner: Vegetarian chili with cornbread (choose gluten-free cornbread if needed)

Snacks: Edamame pods, sliced bell pepper with hummus

DAY 5

Breakfast: Cottage cheese with sliced peaches and a drizzle of honey

Lunch: Veggie wrap with hummus, spinach, bell peppers, and whole-wheat tortilla

Dinner: Tofu poke bowl with brown rice, seaweed salad, edamame, and vegetables

Snacks: Apple slices with almond butter, sliced bell pepper with hummus

DAY 6

Breakfast: Whole-wheat toast with avocado and hard-boiled egg

Lunch: Lentil and quinoa salad with chopped vegetables (tomatoes, cucumber, onions)

Dinner: Salmon salad with mixed greens, avocado, and a lemon dressing

Snacks: Berries with a handful of almonds, carrot sticks with hummus

DAY 7

Breakfast: Overnight oats with berries and chia seeds (soaked in almond milk overnight)

Lunch: Turkey chili with chopped vegetables and cornbread (choose gluten-free cornbread if needed)

Dinner: Vegetarian lasagna with whole-wheat noodles and lentil filling

Snacks: Trail mix with nuts, seeds, and dried fruits, Greek yogurt with berries and chia seeds

WEEK 2

DAY 8

(Repeat any previous day's meals or experiment with a new MIND-friendly recipe)

Opt for a meal you particularly enjoyed or try a new recipe that adheres to the MIND diet principles.

DAY 9

Breakfast: Smoothie with almond milk, banana, spinach, and protein powder

Lunch: Black bean burger on a whole-wheat bun with avocado and side salad

Dinner: Chicken stir-fry with brown rice and vegetables (broccoli, carrots, bell peppers)

Snacks: Edamame pods, hard-boiled egg with cucumber slices

DAY 10

Breakfast: Whole-wheat pancakes with blueberries and walnuts

Lunch: Lentil soup with a side salad and whole-grain bread

Dinner: Baked tofu with roasted vegetables (sweet potato, onion, zucchini) and brown rice

Snacks: Apple slices with almond butter, cottage cheese with pineapple chunks

DAY 11

Breakfast: Scrambled eggs with spinach and salsa

Lunch: Veggie wrap with hummus, spinach, bell peppers, and whole-wheat tortilla

Dinner: Vegetarian chili with cornbread (choose gluten-free cornbread if needed)

Snacks: Berries with a handful of almonds, sliced bell pepper with hummus

DAY 12

Breakfast: Oatmeal with berries and chia seeds

Lunch: Chickpea salad sandwich on whole-wheat bread with avocado and lettuce

Dinner: Salmon with roasted Brussels sprouts and quinoa

Snacks: Trail mix with nuts, seeds, and dried fruits, Greek yogurt with berries and chia seeds

DAY 13

Breakfast: Whole-wheat toast with avocado and hard-boiled egg

Lunch: Lentil soup with whole-wheat bread

Dinner: Black bean burgers on whole-wheat buns with sweet potato fries

Snacks: Apple slices with almond butter, carrot sticks with hummus

DAY 14

Breakfast: Smoothie with almond milk, banana, spinach, and protein powder

Lunch: Salad with grilled chicken, quinoa, and a vinaigrette dressing

Dinner: Fish tacos with grilled fish, corn tortillas, salsa, and avocado

Snacks: Berries with a handful

WEEK 3

DAY 15

Breakfast: Chia pudding with berries and almond milk

Lunch: Tuna salad sandwich on whole-wheat bread with lettuce and tomato

Dinner: Lentil stew with whole-grain bread and side salad

Snacks: Trail mix with nuts, seeds, and dried fruits, cottage cheese with pineapple chunks

DAY 16

Breakfast: Whole-wheat muffin with berries (gluten-free option available)

Lunch: Black bean burgers on whole-wheat buns with sweet potato fries

Dinner: Veggie stir-fry with tofu and brown rice noodles

Snacks: Apple slices with almond butter, sliced bell pepper with hummus

DAY 17

Breakfast: Overnight oats and chia seeds (soaked in almond milk overnight)

Lunch: Chicken stir-fry with brown rice and vegetables (broccoli, carrots, bell peppers)

Dinner: Baked salmon with roasted vegetables (and brown rice

Snacks: Edamame pods, Greek yogurt with berries and chia seeds

DAY 18

Breakfast: Smoothie with almond milk, banana, spinach, and protein powder
Lunch: Lentil and quinoa salad with chopped vegetables (tomatoes, cucumber, onions)
Dinner: Vegetarian lasagna with whole-wheat noodles and lentil filling
Snacks: Berries with a handful of almonds, carrot sticks with hummus

DAY 19

Breakfast: Scrambled eggs with spinach and salsa
Lunch: Chickpea salad sandwich on gluten-free bread with avocado and lettuce (if needed)
Dinner: Baked chicken with roasted vegetables (sweet potatoes, carrots, broccoli) and quinoa
Snacks: Trail mix with nuts, seeds, and dried fruits, apple slices with almond butter

DAY 20

Breakfast: Whole-wheat pancakes with blueberries and walnuts
Lunch: Tofu poke bowl with brown rice, seaweed salad, edamame, and vegetables
Dinner: Salmon salad with mixed greens, avocado, and a lemon dressing
Snacks: Edamame pods, cottage cheese with pineapple chunks

DAY 21

Breakfast: Oatmeal with berries and chia seeds

Lunch: Salad with grilled chicken, quinoa, and a vinaigrette dressing

Dinner: Veggie stir-fry with tofu and brown rice noodles

Snacks: Trail mix with nuts, seeds, and dried fruits, carrot sticks with hummus

WEEK 4

DAY 22

Breakfast: Smoothie with almond milk, banana, spinach, and protein powder
Lunch: Lentil soup with whole-wheat bread

Dinner: Baked tofu with roasted vegetables (sweet potato, onion, zucchini) and brown rice
Snacks: Apple slices with almond butter, berries with a handful of almonds

DAY 23

Breakfast: Whole-wheat toast with avocado and hard-boiled egg

Lunch: Black bean burger on a whole-wheat bun with avocado and side salad

Dinner: Vegetarian chili with cornbread (choose gluten-free cornbread if needed)

Snacks: Trail mix with nuts, seeds, and dried fruits, sliced bell pepper with hummus

DAY 24

Breakfast: Scrambled eggs with spinach and salsa

Lunch: Leftover salmon from dinner with a side of brown rice or quinoa

Dinner: Lentil stew with whole-grain bread and side salad

Snacks: Edamame pods, Greek yogurt with berries and chia seeds

DAY 25

Breakfast: Overnight oats with berries and chia seeds (soaked in almond milk overnight)

Lunch: Chickpea salad sandwich on whole-wheat bread with avocado and lettuce

Dinner: Fish tacos with grilled fish, corn tortillas, salsa, and avocado

Snacks: Apple slices with almond butter, carrot sticks with hummus

DAY 26

Breakfast: Cottage cheese with sliced peaches and a drizzle of honey

Lunch: Whole-wheat pasta salad with vegetables and chickpeas

Dinner: Baked chicken with roasted vegetables (broccoli, carrots, bell peppers) and quinoa

Snacks: Berries with a handful of almonds, sliced bell pepper with hummus

DAY 27

Breakfast: Whole-wheat toast with avocado and hard-boiled egg

Lunch: Veggie wrap with hummus, spinach, bell peppers, and whole-wheat tortilla

Dinner: Vegetarian curry with chickpeas, vegetables (broccoli, cauliflower, carrots) and brown rice

Snacks: Trail

DAY 28

(Repeat any previous day's meals or experiment with a new MIND-friendly recipe)

Opt for a meal you particularly enjoyed or try a new recipe that adheres to the MIND diet principles.

Chapter 5
Embracing Mindful Eating

Mindful eating is a practice rooted in mindfulness, an ancient contemplative tradition that involves paying attention to the present moment with openness, curiosity, and acceptance. When applied to eating, mindful eating involves cultivating awareness of the sensory experiences associated with food, such as sight, smell, taste, texture, and even the sounds of eating. It also involves tuning into hunger and fullness cues, as well as observing emotional and psychological responses to food.

The concept of mindful eating is deeply intertwined with both physical and mental health. On a physical level, mindful eating can promote healthier eating habits by encouraging individuals to savor and appreciate their food, leading to greater satisfaction and enjoyment of meals. By slowing down and being more attentive to hunger and fullness signals, mindful eating can also help prevent overeating and support weight management goals.

Moreover, mindful eating has profound implications for mental health and emotional well-being. By fostering a nonjudgmental attitude toward food and eating, mindful eating can reduce feelings of guilt, shame, or anxiety often associated with food choices. It encourages a compassionate and nurturing relationship with food, allowing individuals to make food choices that align with their values and preferences without falling into restrictive or disordered eating patterns.

Additionally, mindful eating promotes a deeper connection between mind and body, enhancing awareness of how different foods make us feel physically and emotionally. This heightened self-awareness can empower individuals to make more conscious and intentional choices about their dietary habits, leading to greater overall satisfaction and balance in life.

Connecting Mindful Eating to Brain Health

Emerging research suggests a connection between mindful eating and brain health. Studies indicate that mindful eating practices may be associated with:

Improved cognitive function: Enhanced memory, focus, and decision-making abilities.

Reduced risk of cognitive decline: Potentially playing a role in preventing age-related cognitive decline and neurodegenerative diseases.

Increased emotional well-being: Promoting better management of stress, anxiety, and depression.

Practical Tips for Becoming a Mindful Eater

1. Pay Attention to Hunger and Fullness Cues

Before eating, take a moment to check in with your body and assess your hunger levels. Are you truly hungry, or are you eating out of habit, boredom, or emotions? Eat when you're moderately hungry, but not overly ravenous. Aim to stop eating when you're comfortably satisfied, before you feel overly full or stuffed.

Practice mindful eating by pausing midway through your meal to gauge your level of fullness. Take a few deep breaths and ask yourself how hungry you still feel. Adjust your eating pace accordingly.

2. Avoid Distractions While Eating

Minimize distractions during meal times by turning off electronic devices, such as TVs, smartphones, or computers. Create a calm and peaceful eating environment free from external stimuli.

Focus your attention solely on the act of eating, allowing yourself to fully experience the sensory aspects of your meal, including its appearance, aroma, flavor, and texture.

Engage all your senses while eating, savoring each bite mindfully without rushing through your meal. Chew slowly and deliberately, allowing yourself to fully appreciate the taste and texture of your food.

3. Savor the Taste and Texture of Food

Take time to savor each mouthful of food, paying attention to its flavors, aromas, and textures. Notice the different sensations as you chew and swallow.

Experiment with mindful eating exercises, such as mindful tasting or mindful eating meditations, to deepen your sensory awareness and appreciation of food.

Express gratitude for the nourishment and pleasure that food provides, cultivating a sense of reverence and appreciation for the act of eating.

4. Manage Stress Around Eating

Practice stress management techniques, such as deep breathing, meditation, or progressive muscle relaxation, before meals to promote a calm and relaxed state of mind.

Avoid using food as a coping mechanism for stress or emotional discomfort. Instead, find healthier ways to manage stress, such as going for a walk, journaling, or talking to a supportive friend.

Be compassionate with yourself if you notice stress or emotional eating patterns emerging. Practice self-compassion and self-care, seeking support from a therapist or counselor if needed.

By incorporating these practical tips into your daily eating habits, you can cultivate mindfulness in your relationship with food, leading to greater satisfaction, enjoyment, and overall well-being. Mindful eating not only nourishes your body but also nurtures your mind and spirit, fostering a deeper sense of connection and appreciation for the nourishing power of food.

Chapter 6
Mind Diet Recipe Collection

Here is a collection of mind diet recipes you can choose from to make your own personalized food menu.

Dessert Recipes

1. Mixed Berry Chia Seed Pudding: Combine chia seeds, almond milk, and mixed berries in a jar, then refrigerate overnight for a creamy and antioxidant-rich dessert option.

2. Dark Chocolate Avocado Mousse: Blend ripe avocado with cocoa powder, maple syrup, and a splash of almond milk until smooth, then chill until set for a rich and indulgent treat.

3. Baked Apple Slices with Cinnamon: Slice apples and toss with cinnamon, then bake until tender for a naturally sweet and comforting dessert.

4. Banana Walnut Bites: Slice bananas and top with a dollop of almond butter and a sprinkle of crushed walnuts for a simple and satisfying sweet snack.

5. Greek Yogurt with Honey and Pistachios: Serve Greek yogurt with a drizzle of honey and a handful of chopped pistachios for a creamy, protein-rich dessert option.

6. Frozen Berry Yogurt Bark: Spread Greek yogurt onto a baking sheet, then top with mixed berries and freeze until set for a refreshing and nutritious frozen treat.

7. Chocolate-Dipped Strawberries: Dip fresh strawberries into melted dark chocolate, then chill until the chocolate hardens for a decadent and antioxidant-packed dessert.

Snack Recipes

1. Veggie Sticks with Hummus: Serve sliced carrots, cucumbers, bell peppers, and cherry tomatoes with hummus for a crunchy and nutrient-packed snack option.

2. Almond Butter Banana Bites: Spread almond butter onto banana slices, then top with a sprinkle of cinnamon and a few dark chocolate chips for a satisfying and energy-boosting snack.

3. Trail Mix: Mix together nuts, seeds, dried fruit, and dark chocolate chips for a portable and nutrient-dense snack option.

4. Cottage Cheese with Pineapple: Serve cottage cheese with fresh pineapple chunks for a protein-rich and refreshing snack.

5. Roasted Chickpeas: Toss chickpeas with olive oil, salt, and your favorite spices, then roast until crispy for a crunchy and protein-packed snack option.

6. Ants on a Log: Spread celery sticks with almond butter and top with raisins for a fun and nutritious snack option.

7. Apple Slices with Almond Butter: Serve apple slices with almond butter for a satisfying and fiber-rich snack.

Side Dish Recipes

1. Garlic Roasted Brussels Sprouts: Toss halved Brussels sprouts with olive oil, minced garlic, salt, and pepper, then roast until caramelized and tender for a delicious and nutrient-dense side dish.

2. Lemon Herb Quinoa: Cook quinoa according to package instructions, then toss with lemon zest, chopped herbs, and a drizzle of olive oil for a flavorful and protein-packed side dish.

3. Steamed Broccoli with Parmesan: Steam broccoli florets until tender, then sprinkle with grated Parmesan cheese and a squeeze of lemon juice for a simple and nutritious side dish.

4. Grilled Asparagus with Balsamic Glaze: Grill asparagus spears until charred and tender, then drizzle with balsamic glaze for a flavorful and antioxidant-rich side dish.

5. Roasted Sweet Potatoes with Rosemary: Toss sweet potato cubes with olive oil, minced rosemary, salt, and pepper, then roast until golden and caramelized for a savory and vitamin-rich side dish.

6. Quinoa Salad with Roasted Vegetables: Toss cooked quinoa with roasted vegetables like bell peppers, zucchini, and cherry tomatoes, then drizzle with balsamic vinaigrette for a colorful and nutritious side dish.

7. Caprese Salad: Arrange sliced tomatoes, fresh mozzarella cheese, and basil leaves on a platter, then drizzle with balsamic glaze and a sprinkle of sea salt for a classic and refreshing side dish.

🍽 Main Dish Recipes 🍽

1. Grilled Salmon with Lemon and Dill: Season salmon fillets with fresh dill, lemon juice, and olive oil, then grill until cooked through for a protein-rich and omega-3-packed main dish.

2. Mediterranean Stuffed Bell Peppers: Fill bell peppers with a mixture of cooked quinoa, chickpeas, diced tomatoes, olives, and feta cheese, then bake until bubbly and golden for a flavorful and vegetarian-friendly meal.

3. Lemon Garlic Shrimp Scampi: Sauté shrimp with minced garlic, lemon zest, and white wine, then toss with cooked whole wheat pasta for a light and flavorful main dish.

4. Turkey and Vegetable Stir-Fry: Stir-fry lean turkey breast strips with mixed vegetables and a savory sauce, then serve over brown rice or quinoa for a protein-packed and nutrient-rich meal.

5. Chicken and Vegetable Skewers: Thread chicken breast cubes and colorful vegetables onto skewers, then grill until charred and cooked through for a simple and nutritious main dish.

6. Lentil and Vegetable Curry: Simmer lentils with diced vegetables, coconut milk, and curry spices until tender and flavorful for a hearty and plant-based main dish.

7. Eggplant Parmesan: Layer sliced eggplant with marinara sauce, mozzarella cheese, and Parmesan cheese, then bake until bubbly and golden for a comforting and vegetarian-friendly main dish.

Soup Recipes

1. Minestrone Soup: Simmer diced vegetables, beans, whole wheat pasta, and vegetable broth with Italian herbs and spices for a hearty and nutrient-packed soup.

2. Butternut Squash Soup: Roast butternut squash until tender, then blend with vegetable broth, garlic, and spices for a creamy and comforting soup option.

3. Spinach and White Bean Soup: Sauté onion, garlic, and diced vegetables until softened, then add vegetable broth, canned white beans, and chopped spinach for a protein-rich and nourishing soup.

4. Lentil Vegetable Soup: Simmer lentils with diced vegetables like carrots, celery, and onions in a flavorful broth seasoned with herbs and spices for a hearty and nutritious soup.

5. Tomato Basil Soup: Blend roasted tomatoes with garlic, onions, basil, and vegetable broth for a comforting and immune-boosting soup option.

6. Chicken and Rice Soup: Simmer shredded chicken breast with cooked rice, diced vegetables, and chicken broth for a classic and comforting soup option.

7. Cauliflower and Leek Soup: Sauté leeks and cauliflower until tender, then blend with vegetable broth and seasonings for a creamy and low-carb soup option.

🥗 Salad Recipes 🥗

1. Greek Salad: Toss chopped cucumbers, tomatoes, red onion, Kalamata olives, and feta cheese with a lemon-oregano vinaigrette for a refreshing and Mediterranean-inspired salad.

2. Quinoa and Chickpea Salad: Combine cooked quinoa with canned chickpeas, diced bell peppers, cherry tomatoes, cucumber, and parsley, then toss with a lemon-tahini dressing for a protein-packed and fiber-rich salad.

3. Spinach and Strawberry Salad: Toss fresh spinach with sliced strawberries, goat cheese, almonds, and a balsamic vinaigrette for a sweet and savory salad option.

4. Beet and Arugula Salad: Roast beets until tender, then toss with arugula, goat cheese, walnuts, and a citrus vinaigrette for a colorful and nutrient-dense salad.

5. Caprese Quinoa Salad: Combine cooked quinoa with cherry tomatoes, fresh mozzarella balls, basil leaves, and balsamic glaze for a light and refreshing salad option.

6. Kale and Blueberry Salad: Massage kale leaves with lemon juice and olive oil until tender, then toss with fresh blueberries, crumbled feta cheese, and toasted almonds for a vibrant and antioxidant-rich salad.

7. Broccoli Cranberry Salad: Blanch broccoli florets until tender-crisp, then toss with dried cranberries, sunflower seeds, red onion, and a creamy yogurt dressing for a crunchy and flavorful salad.

Smoothies

1. Berry Spinach Smoothie:

Ingredients : 1 cup fresh spinach leaves, 1/2 cup mixed berries (such as strawberries, blueberries, and raspberries, 1/2 banana, 1/2 cup Greek yogurt, 1/2 cup almond milk, 1 tablespoon chia seeds (optional)

Instructions:

1. Combine all ingredients in a blender.
2. Blend until smooth and creamy.
3. Serve immediately and enjoy this antioxidant-rich smoothie.

2. Green Mango Smoothie:

Ingredients: 1 cup fresh spinach leaves, 1/2 cup frozen mango chunks, 1/2 banana, 1/2 cup Greek yogurt, 1/2 cup coconut water, 1 tablespoon honey (optional)

Instructions:

1. Place all ingredients in a blender.
2. Blend until smooth and creamy.
3. Taste and adjust sweetness with honey, if desired.
4. Pour into glasses and serve chilled.

3. Blueberry Avocado Smoothie:

Ingredients: 1/2 cup blueberries (fresh or frozen), 1/2 avocado, 1/2 cup Greek yogurt, 1/2 cup almond milk, 1 tablespoon honey or maple syrup

Instructions:

1. Combine all ingredients in a blender.
2. Blend until smooth and creamy.
3. Sweeten with honey or maple syrup to taste.
4. Pour into glasses and enjoy this creamy and antioxidant-packed smoothie.

4. Pineapple Kale Smoothie:

Ingredients: 1 cup kale leaves, 1/2 cup frozen pineapple chunks, 1/2 banana, 1/2 cup Greek yogurt, 1/2 cup coconut water or almond milk

Instructions:

1. Add all ingredients to a blender.
2. Blend until smooth and well combined.
3. Adjust consistency with more coconut water or almond milk if needed.
4. Pour into glasses and serve immediately.

5. Banana Walnut Smoothie:

*Ingredients:*1 ripe banana, 1/4 cup walnuts, 1/2 cup Greek yogurt, 1/2 cup almond milk, 1 tablespoon honey or maple syrup (optional)

Instructions:
1. Place all ingredients in a blender.
2. Blend until smooth and creamy.
3. Sweeten with honey or maple syrup if desired.
4. Pour into glasses and garnish with additional walnuts if desired.

6. Coconut Berry Smoothie:

Ingredients: 1/2 cup mixed berries (such as strawberries, blueberries, and raspberries), 1/2 cup Greek yogurt, 1/2 cup coconut milk, 1/2 cup coconut water, 1 tablespoon shredded coconut (optional)

Instructions:
1. Combine all ingredients in a blender.
2. Blend until smooth and creamy.
3. Add more coconut water if needed to reach desired consistency.
4. Pour into glasses and sprinkle with shredded coconut if desired.

7. Cherry Almond Smoothie:

Ingredients: 1/2 cup cherries (fresh or frozen), 1/4 cup almonds, 1/2 cup Greek yogurt, 1/2 cup almond milk, 1 tablespoon honey or maple syrup (optional)

Instructions
1. Add all ingredients to a blender.
2. Blend until smooth and creamy.
3. Sweeten with honey or maple syrup if desired.
4. Pour into glasses and enjoy this delicious and protein-rich smoothie.

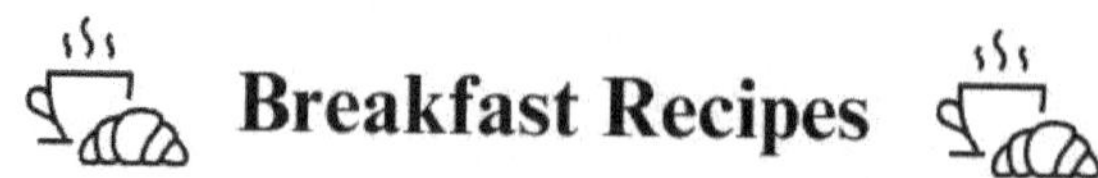 Breakfast Recipes

1. Greek Yogurt Parfait with Berries and Granola: Layer Greek yogurt with mixed berries and granola in a glass or bowl for a protein-rich and satisfying breakfast option.

2. Vegetable Frittata: Whisk eggs with diced vegetables like bell peppers, onions, spinach, and tomatoes, then bake until set for a hearty and nutrient-packed breakfast.

3. Oatmeal with Mixed Berries and Almonds: Cook rolled oats with almond milk, then top with mixed berries, sliced almonds, and a drizzle of honey for a comforting and fiber-rich breakfast option.

4. Avocado Toast with Poached Eggs: Mash avocado onto whole grain toast, then top with poached eggs and a sprinkle of red pepper flakes for a savory and protein-packed breakfast option.

5. Smoothie Bowl: Blend frozen mixed berries with Greek yogurt and spinach until smooth, then top with sliced fruit, granola, and a drizzle of honey for a refreshing and nutrient-packed breakfast option.

6. Breakfast Burrito: Fill a whole wheat tortilla with scrambled eggs, black beans, diced vegetables, and salsa for a portable and protein-rich breakfast option.

7. Overnight Chia Seed Pudding: Mix chia seeds with almond milk and vanilla extract, then refrigerate overnight until thickened for a creamy and protein-packed breakfast option.

Lunch Recipes

1. Quinoa Salad with Grilled Chicken: Combine cooked quinoa with grilled chicken breast, diced vegetables, feta cheese, and a lemon-herb vinaigrette for a protein-packed and satisfying lunch option.

2. Tuna Salad Stuffed Avocado: Mix canned tuna with Greek yogurt, diced celery, and lemon juice, then serve in halved avocado shells for a creamy and protein-rich lunch option.

3. Turkey and Hummus Wrap: Spread whole grain tortillas with hummus, then fill with sliced turkey breast, shredded lettuce, cucumber, and tomato for a satisfying and protein-packed lunch option.

4. Mediterranean Chickpea Salad: Toss canned chickpeas with diced cucumber, cherry tomatoes, olives, red onion, feta cheese, and a lemon-tahini dressing for a flavorful and protein-rich lunch option.

5. Veggie and Hummus Sandwich: Spread whole grain bread with hummus, then layer with sliced vegetables like cucumber, bell pepper, tomato, and avocado for a crunchy and fiber-rich lunch option.

6. Lentil and Vegetable Soup: Simmer lentils with diced vegetables like carrots, celery, and onions in a flavorful broth seasoned with herbs and spices for a hearty and nutritious lunch option.

7. Quinoa and Black Bean Salad: Combine cooked quinoa with canned black beans, diced bell peppers, corn, avocado, and cilantro, then toss with a lime-cumin vinaigrette for a protein-packed and satisfying lunch option.

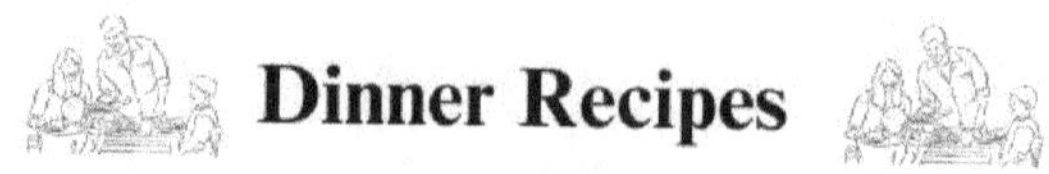 **Dinner Recipes**

1. Baked Salmon with Lemon and Dill: Season salmon fillets with fresh dill, lemon juice, and olive oil, then bake until cooked through for a protein-rich and omega-3-packed main dish.

2. Mediterranean Stuffed Bell Peppers: Fill bell peppers with a mixture of cooked quinoa, chickpeas, diced tomatoes, olives, and feta cheese, then bake until bubbly and golden for a flavorful and vegetarian-friendly meal.

3. Lemon Garlic Shrimp Scampi: Sauté shrimp with minced garlic, lemon zest, and white wine, then toss with cooked whole wheat pasta for a light and flavorful main dish.

4. Turkey and Vegetable Stir Fry: Stir-fry lean turkey breast strips with mixed vegetables and a savory sauce, then serve over brown rice or quinoa for a protein-packed and nutrient-rich meal.

5. Chicken and Vegetable Skewers: Thread chicken breast cubes and colorful vegetables onto skewers, then grill until charred and cooked through for a simple and nutritious main dish.

6. Lentil and Vegetable Curry: Simmer lentils with diced vegetables, coconut milk, and curry spices until tender and flavorful for a hearty and plant-based main dish.

7. Eggplant Parmesan: Layer sliced eggplant with marinara sauce, mozzarella cheese, and Parmesan cheese, then bake until bubbly and golden for a comforting and vegetarian-friendly main dish.

These recipes offer a variety of options for incorporating brain-boosting foods into your diet while adhering to the principles of the MIND diet. Enjoy experimenting with these flavorful and nutritious dishes for a healthier and happier lifestyle!

Chapter 7
Additional Resources and Support

Welcome to Chapter 7 of our guide! In this final chapter, we delve into additional resources and support systems that can further enhance your journey towards a healthier mind and body. While adopting the MIND diet and incorporating brain-boosting foods into your lifestyle is a significant step towards improving cognitive function and overall well-being, having access to additional resources and support can provide valuable guidance, motivation, and encouragement along the way.

In this chapter, we've curated a selection of resources that encompass various aspects of health and wellness, from educational materials and cookbooks to online communities and support groups. Whether you're seeking more information on the science behind nutrition and brain health, looking for inspiration and ideas for MIND diet-friendly recipes, or hoping to connect with like-minded individuals on a similar wellness journey, you'll find a wealth of resources here to support you every step of the way.

We understand that making dietary and lifestyle changes can sometimes feel overwhelming or daunting, which is why having a supportive network and access to reliable information can be invaluable. Our aim with this chapter is to empower you with the tools, knowledge, and support you need to make sustainable and positive changes for your mental and physical health.

So, without further ado, let's explore the additional resources and support systems that can help you thrive on your MIND diet journey!

Resources for Further Exploration

MIND Diet

1. **Rush University Medical Center:** https://www.rush.edu/news/mind-diet - Explore the official website of the MIND diet research, providing detailed information, research findings, and recipes.

2. **National Institute on Aging:** https://www.soulfoodsalon.com/post/comparing-the-mind-and-mediterranean-diets-by-christina-badaracco-mph-rd - Gain insights into the MIND diet compared to the Mediterrancan dict from a reliable government resource.

3. **Harvard T.H. Chan School of Public Health:** https://www.hsph.harvard.edu/nutritionsource/healthy-weight/diet-reviews/mind-diet/ - Access this reputable source for a brief overview and potential benefits of the MIND diet.

Mental Health:

1. **National Institute of Mental Health:** https://www.nimh.nih.gov/health - This comprehensive website from the National Institutes of Health offers various resources on mental health topics, including informative articles, educational materials, and support groups.

2. MentalHealth.gov: https://www.samhsa.gov/mental-health - A government website providing general information about mental health, including definitions, signs and symptoms of different mental health conditions, and access to mental health services.

3. National Alliance on Mental Illness (NAMI): https://www.nami.org/Home - This leading mental health advocacy organization offers support, education, and resources for individuals and families affected by mental illness.

Healthy Eating:

1. Academy of Nutrition and Dietetics: https://www.eatright.org/ - This website from the leading professional organization for registered dietitians provides reliable information on various dietary topics, including healthy eating tips, meal planning resources, and finding a registered dietitian.

2. ChooseMyPlate (.gov): https://www.myplate.gov/ - This government website offers a user-friendly guide to healthy eating, including information on food groups, portion sizes, and building a balanced diet.

3. The World Health Organization (WHO): https://www.who.int/news-room/fact-sheets/detail/healthy-diet - Access the WHO's website for information on healthy eating patterns, global recommendations, and strategies for promoting healthy diets.

Additional Resources

Mindful Eating Books:
1. "Full Catastrophe Living" by Jon Kabat-Zinn
2. "Mindful Eating: A Guide to Rediscovering Your Body's Wisdom" by Jean Kristeller

Mindful Eating Apps:
1. Headspace,
2. Calm,
3. Shine

Cookbooks:

Find cookbooks dedicated to the MIND diet or healthy eating in general, offering recipe inspiration and guidance for incorporating these principles into your meals. Here are some professional cookbooks that focus on the MIND Diet:

1. **The Ultimate MIND Diet Cookbook:** 100 Recipes to Help Prevent Alzheimer's and Dementia by Natalie Digiulio, MS, RD. This cookbook features 100 MIND Diet-specific recipes that are both delicious and nutritious. The recipes are also categorized by meal type, making it easy to find what you're looking for.

2. **The MIND Diet Plan and Cookbook:** Recipes and Lifestyle Guidelines to Help Prevent Alzheimer's and Dementia by Julie Andrews, MS, RDN, CD. This book not only provides over 100 MIND Diet recipes, but it also includes information about the science behind the MIND Diet and tips for implementing it into your lifestyle.

3. **The Brain Health Cookbook:** MIND Diet Recipes to Prevent Disease and Enhance Cognitive Power by Julie Andrews, MS, RDN, CD. This cookbook focuses on recipes that are not only delicious but also promote brain health. The recipes are categorized by brain function, such as memory, focus, and mood.

It's important to note that while these cookbooks can be a helpful resource, it's always a good idea to talk to your doctor or a registered dietitian before making any changes to your diet.

Support Groups

Finding a support group can be a valuable step in your mental health journey. Connecting with others who understand your experiences can provide emotional support, validation, and a sense of community. Here are some resources to help you find a suitable group:

National Organizations:

1. National Alliance on Mental Illness (NAMI): https://www.nami.org/Home offers peer-led support groups across the US. Find local chapters and group options (including virtual groups) through their website.

2. MentalHealth.gov: https://www.samhsa.gov/ provides information on various mental health topics, including a directory of national support organizations, some of which offer online or local support groups.

3. The Jed Foundation: https://jedfoundation.org/ specifically focuses on supporting emotional health and preventing suicide among teens and young adults. Their website offers resources for finding support groups in your area.

Online Resources:

1.Support Groups Central: https://www.supportgroupscentral.com/admin/ is a comprehensive directory of online and in-person support groups for various conditions, including mental health concerns.

2. MeetUp: [https://www.meetup.com/] can be a great way to find local groups focused on specific mental health interests, such as anxiety support or depression support groups.

3. Facebook Groups: Many private and public Facebook groups cater to various mental health conditions. Search for groups relevant to your specific needs while practicing caution and ensuring the group is moderated and adheres to community guidelines.

Remember

This list is not exhaustive, and it's crucial to consult with a healthcare professional before making significant changes to your diet or mental health routine. They can provide personalized guidance and recommendations best suited for your individual needs and medical history.

Conclusion

As you reach the end of this book, it's not a goodbye but rather a "welcome" to a new chapter in your life. The MIND diet and the practice of mindful eating offer you not just a dietary plan, but a transformative journey towards nourishing your body and mind.

Throughout these pages, you've delved into the science-backed benefits of the MIND diet, explored the powerful principles of mindful eating, and discovered a treasure trove of delicious and brain-healthy recipes. Remember, this is just the beginning. Implementing these practices takes time and dedication. Be patient with yourself, celebrate your progress, and don't be discouraged by occasional setbacks. Embrace the journey as an ongoing exploration, continually learning and refining your approach.

The MIND diet guidelines serve as a foundation but feel empowered to personalize your experience. Experiment with recipes, adapt them to your preferences and explore additional healthy ingredients that resonate with your taste buds and cultural background.

As you embark on this journey of mindful eating and brain health, remember the power of sharing. Spread awareness about the MIND diet and mindful eating practices with your loved ones, encouraging them to explore these paths for their own well-being. Together, we can create a ripple effect of positive choices that foster individual and collective well-being.

The future holds immense potential for continued discoveries in the field of brain health and nutrition. As research evolves, so too can your approach. Stay curious, remain engaged, and continue to nourish your body and mind with the tools and knowledge you've gained. Remember, you hold the key to unlocking a life filled with vibrant health, cognitive resilience, and joyful engagement with the world around you.

May your journey towards a healthier brain and a mindful approach to food be filled with delicious discoveries, personal growth, and a renewed sense of empowerment. Bon appétit and good health!

With warmest regards,
JOAN JONES

Your Review Matters!

Dear Reader

Thank you for taking this journey with me through the exploration of the MIND diet and mindful eating. I hope this book has equipped you with valuable knowledge and delicious recipes to embark on your own path to brain health and well-being.

Your feedback is crucial in helping me improve future editions and reach a wider audience who could benefit from these practices. Would you be willing to share your honest review on the platform.

Even a few words can make a significant difference. Your review can help others discover this resource and empower them to prioritize their brain health.

Thank you for your support and engagement!

With gratitude,
JOAN JONES

EXPLORE OTHER BOOKS BY JOAN JONES

Dear Reader,

We hope you have found "Mind Diet Advanced" by Joan Jones to be a transformative and enlightening experience. As you delve into the principles and insights shared in this remarkable guide, you are likely discovering new ways to enhance your cognitive health and overall well-being. Joan Jones's profound understanding of nutrition and its impact on the mind is evident in every chapter, making this book an invaluable resource for anyone seeking to optimize their mental performance and longevity.

If you have been inspired by the knowledge and practical advice in "Mind Diet Advanced," we warmly encourage you to explore more of Joan Jones's works. Her extensive expertise and passion for empowering individuals through health and wellness are reflected across her diverse range of publications. Each book is meticulously researched and written with the same dedication to improving the quality of life for her readers.

We encourage you to take the next step on your journey towards a healthier mind and body by delving into these enriching books. Joan Jones's commitment to her readers' health is unwavering, and her works are a testament to her dedication to helping you achieve your wellness goals.

Happy reading, and may your journey to better health be both enlightening and rewarding.

With gratitude,
JOAN JONES